Fred Tozer's
NEWTON ABBOT
album II

OBELISK PUBLICATIONS

Other Books in this Series

Fred Tozer's Newton Abbot Album
Peter Tully's Pictures of Paignton
Peter Tully's Pictures of Paignton Part II
Peter Tully's Pictures of Paignton Part III
Albert Labbett's Crediton Collection
Albert Labbett's Crediton Collection II
An Alphington Album, P. Aplin & J. Gaskell
The Dawlish Collection, Bernard Chapman
The Totnes Collection, Bill Bennett
Ian Jubb's Exeter Collection
Mike & Hilary Wreford's Okehampton Collection
Mike & Hilary Wreford's Okehampton Collection II
Mike & Hilary Wreford's Okehampton Collection III
Pictorial Torquay, Leslie Retallick
Kingsteignton Collection, Richard Harris
A Chudleigh Collection
A Brixham Album
An Exeter Boyhood, Frank Retter
The Pubs and Inns of Ashburton, Pete Webb

For further details of these or any of our extensive Devon titles, please contact us at 2 Church Hill, Pinhoe, Exeter, EX4 9ER, Tel: (01392) 468556.

ISBN: 1 899073 11 6

Acknowledgements

Thanks to Mr and Mrs Daniels, Mr and Mrs Martin for copying family photos; Arthur King for blitz and tank pictures; Ivor Ellis, Mr and Mrs Short for additional information; Stephen McKay for copying old photos. Thanks also to Nicholas Horne for picture on page 4; Tony Paddon; Nicholas Toyne (Jerome Dessain) page 31 (top right); Chips Barber for providing various pictures, also page 16 (bottom right), page 38, page 39 (top right)

First Published in 1995 by Obelisk Publications
2 Church Hill, Pinhoe, Exeter, Devon
Designed by Chips and Sally Barber
Typeset by Sally Barber
Printed in Great Britain by
Maslands Ltd, Tiverton, Devon

© Fred Tozer/Obelisk Publications

All Rights Reserved. No part of this publication may be reproduced, stored in a retrieval system, or transmitted, in any form or by any means, electronic, mechanical, photocopying, recording or otherwise, without the prior permission of the publishers and copyright holders.

Welcome to Newton Abbot! Following the success of the first Newton Abbot Album I have 'unearthed' some more pictures of our town that may bring back a few memories of what the town and the townsfolk were like in years gone by. Even this composite card reveals how times have changed as some of the views on it have changed considerably but not beyond recognition like many to be found later in this book. I hope you enjoy this journey down 'Memory Lane'.

To many people the name of Newton Abbot is synonymous with horse racing. For years the course, built on Teign Marshes, has drawn crowds from far afield to enjoy the racing. Since this picture was taken, the area in the vicinity of the course has changed considerably with the land towards Kingsteignton seeing much development. Opposite is an aerial view looking down on Bradley Lane with Vicary's Wool Mills and Tanyard dominating the scene. This was taken before Brownhills Road was built, Coronation Road coming to an abrupt end here. The River Lemon can be seen 'squeezing' its way through the right hand side of the picture!

4

Baker's Park, Newton Abbot.

Baker's Park is in the bottom right of the last picture but here is shown in all its glory as it looked about 1915. A gathering of young men is evident, the godpost a telltale sign of their intended activities. The park is named after Mr R. H. M. Baker who was once Clerk to the Local Board. In the background of this picture, Mackrell's Almshouses can be seen.

Mackrell's Almshouses, along the south side of Totnes Road, were endowed by Thomas Mackrell, hence their name. The original terrace was built in 1874 and over the middle of the block is an inscription "By the Grace of God the Mackrell Almshouses Erected and Endowed In the year of our Lord 1874". When Thomas died his fortune was inherited by his sister, Miss Sophia Mackrell, and when she passed away, in 1894, the money reverted back to the trustees and more almshouses were added here. These were built in the same style and have their very own inscription. For those who enjoy trivial snippets of information, they may like to know that Thomas Mackrell's parents once kept the old Bell Inn that was in Bank Street!

For many years the traders of Newton Abbot's town centre lived in fear of flood and tempest. The River Lemon rises high on the moors of Dartmoor at a point close to Haytor. Dartmoor is notorious for its high rainfall amounts and a Dartmoor deluge or downpour is enough to send its many rivers shooting seawards in a flash flood frenzy. From this elevated kingdom the Lemon has a sharper profile than most and any obstruction in its wake is liable to create a flood. The Lemon always found it difficult, at such times, to get past Newton Abbot without causing any watery mischief. Although there have been many floods down through the years, these two pictures are from just one of them that occurred in 1938. The picture on the left shows traffic near Lloyds Bank Corner whilst the horizontal view, below, shows a person, who should have invested in a pair of wellington boots, splashing through the flood waters outside Ham & Huddy's shop heading towards the Odeon.
A lot of flood preventive works have been carried out farther upstream and it's believed, and hoped, that the threat of a flash flood on the moor is not one that's likely to inundate the centre of Newton Abbot like it used to, so regularly, in the past.

Courtenay Street has always been an important one in Newton Abbot and it has seen the changes. These pictures are from the early days. The snow scene is from the Great Blizzard of 1891 when most of Devon was brought to a stand (or slip!) still for some six weeks, the blizzard having started in early March that year. The other two pictures show an almost traffic-free society. Today, pedestrianisation has gone some of the way to recreate that same relaxed atmosphere for shoppers in Courtenay Street. However, the major difference is that today it's the rest of the town centre's roads that are constantly congested.

The Globe Hotel stands on this corner of Courtenay Street. And it's highly unlikely that its employees ever imagined that one day, many years later, that this would be a shop. But times change and there have been many in this street, particularly in recent times. The shop of Wm T. White (now Austin's), is on the right, at 6 & 8 Courtenay Street. They were drapers and milliners and we really must take our hats off to them for the quality of their service to customers. Apparently they did everything they could to ensure that not only those who called at the shop for their wares were well looked after but also those who liked to shop by post. Their advert went to great lengths to state that "Special attention is given to Orders by Post and are executed the same day as received." The scene has changed a great deal and another, more recent, addition is the old iron gates from Newton Abbot's Cattle Market, now found at either end of this pedestrianised street.

Courteney Street. Newton Abbot.

Looking the other way from the other end of Courtenay Street, this 1910 view contains many buildings that are no longer with us. As I noted in the first 'Newton Abbot Album' there seems to be a distinct inconsistency in the spelling of the street name. This particular postcard was sent to a married daughter living in Laurence, Massachusetts from her Mother in Newton Abbot to wish her a Happy Birthday – she'd be a bit old and grey now!

The year was 1919 and the townspeople turned out in force to inspect this trophy of war. This German tank and two field guns were brought back to Newton Abbot. The tank was later removed to Baker's Park where it stayed until the Second World War. Then, of course, it was taken as scrap metal, melted down and … wasn't seen again!

Newton Abbot, like many places in Devon, saw its share of action during the Second World War and these two pictures show that many buildings were damaged even though the real target of most attacks, particularly the early ones, was the railway station. The horizontal picture shows us the damage inflicted on South Devon Terrace in a raid that caused the loss of 15 lives in early August 1940. On this site there are now premises of the Readers' Digest. The upright picture shows the bomb-damaged Mount Pleasant after an attack in late April 1942.

Stover Canal and Locks, from Breakneck.

Newton Abbot is a town of hills and so it's hardly surprising to stumble across a number of view cards taken from the top of them. Today a card like this, showing such an industrial scene, would probably never be published. It features the view from what locals refer to as 'Breakneck'. This is the steepest part of the eastern edge of Knowles Hill. The Stover Canal runs into the Whitelake Channel on the left side beside the railway line. This is the goods line that runs up to Heathfield and at one time, when it was also a passenger line, it was possible to go on through Bovey Tracey and Lustleigh to the railway terminus of Moretonhampstead many hundreds of feet higher. It was also possible to get to Exeter via the Teign Valley branch line that ran from the junction station of Heathfield. A close examination of the picture shows that barges can be seen to the left in the canal basin.

14

Pouderham Road is another of those notoriously steep inclines found in Newton Abbot. Several houses on the right of this picture were demolished to make for Newfoundland Way, a road created to be part of the traffic merry-go-round.

Newton Abbot, Great Western Station.

Here we have three very different views of Newton Abbot's railway station. The oldest one is from an age when the horse and carriage were still important and were here in numbers awaiting the arrival of trains. Despite the number of horses, and the combined amounts of time they spent there waiting, the station approaches are remarkably clean and tidy! The station was rebuilt in 1926 and the larger buildings, at the same location, are shown here. The Great Western Railway was at the helm of the proceedings. The clock shows at ten to six, the height of the rush hour but the ladies crossing the road don't seem to be too perturbed by the notion. Cars, that today would be worth a small fortune, await the arrival of trains in this view. The more recent picture was probably taken when there was a strike as there seems to be little happening.

The railways were important to the economy of the town and at their peak about 600 men were employed in a variety of jobs that included painters, trimmers, engineers, boiler makers, fitters and labourers. The scale of the railway operations were enough to earn Newton Abbot the title the "Swindon of the West".

On the opposite page is a picture of Elson's Railway Hotel, from an age when it was the norm for the name of the establishment to be preceeded by the owner's name. The first buildings to be built in Queen Street were the ones in the terrace adjacent to this hotel.

Hey presto! The Elson's Railway Hotel, of the last picture, has become Phillips's Railway Hotel. The picture is packed with characters all, bar a few, wearing some form of head apparel for their celebratory photo. Most have also got buttonholes. The pub has been decorated with flags to suggest a Coronation party may be about to occur. An accordion player, in the front row, is possibly waiting to entertain the others. Even the dog is posing for this picture that goes back many decades.

A swift telephone call, via the operator, to Newton Abbot 37 would have got you through to Balls Ltd, a firm that operated their open top charabancs from premises next to Bearne's School in Queen Street.

I featured three other pictures of Bulpin's in the first volume of this series of books. However "The Pride of the Moor" rides again in this edition with this group of ladies, and a boy, wearing some very fetching hats. Bulpin's started out as ironmongers at 1, Bank Street. About 1916 they entered the motor trade. By 1919 they had a garage in East Street and in 1921-22 the enterprise expanded to a new garage and showroom at 64 Wolborough Street.

To keep the fleet of vehicles on the road and in pristine condition there were the mechanics and other members of staff. In the upright photo the man in the centre is Mr Ron Stoyle with two of the other employees. The firm was also well-known for its car sales and its garage. This upright picture show Bulpin's showrooms and workshop when they were in East Street, next to the Jolly Abbot pub. They were later bought out by Wadham Stringer, now Wadham Kenning.

There is a definite antique charm about these three different commercial vehicles from a Newton Abbot of yesteryear. W. Cross & Co are a firm that still trade in East Street. The two men posed in front of Heywood's van are very smartly attired and even from those early days there was a realisation that advertising on the side of a trade vehicle was a worthwhile exercise! Through their years of existence the company probably dispatched vast amounts of Devonshire clotted cream to other parts of the country and even abroad. The 'Shell' picture was taken in 1939 at Forde Road. The delivery men had a regular run over Milber Down, through St Marychurch and onto Oddicombe Beach where they supplied the fuel for the motor launches that took visitors on 'trips around the bay'. The solid tyres, no doubt, made for an interesting journey to Torquay!

The photo opposite is of Newton Abbot Fair that traditionally took place in the first week of September. The light-coloured houses, just beyond the pens of the cattle market, are those that lie along Halcyon Road.

THE GOODS AND
PRICES OF
A. BLEWETT
& Co.,
WHOLESALE & RETAIL
Stationers and
Tobacconists,
Queen St. Post Office,
NEWTON ABBOT.

Large Stock of
Note-papers, Envelopes,
Fountain & Stylographic
Pens, Ink, Guu,
Initial Stationery, Purses, and
Fancy Goods &c., &c.

Dish Papers, Playing Cards, Tobaccos, Cigars, and Cigarettes, in best condition at rock bottom prices.

DAILY, WEEKLY, AND MONTHLY PAPERS AND PERIODICALS delivered to all parts.

☞ The only Tobacconist giving away Coupons with Tobaccos, &c.
OVER 200 PRESENTS TO CHOOSE FROM.

Here we have two very similar views of Queen Street taken from slightly different angles. Although there are similarities there are also some striking differences that you might like to observe for yourself. The left picture shows the Imperial Electric Theatre with a few potential customers possibly looking at what was on there that day. To the left is a name that we came across earlier with the charabancs and that is the name of Ball's on an end facing wall. On the left is a sign advertising the Empire that was a short distance away at the Recreation Ground.

The picture opposite is a much later one looking up Queen Street from its junction with The Avenue. At the base of the lamppost on the right was a drinking fountain, with water issuing from a lion's head. For those in need of quenching their thirsts metal cups, attached by chains, served the purpose.

Queen Street, Newton Abbot.

Newton Abbot, Queen Street

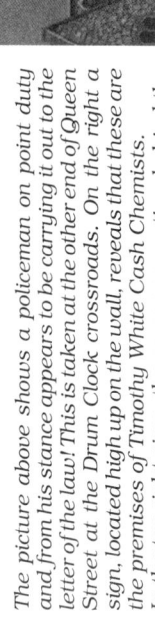

The picture above shows a policeman on point duty and from his stance appears to be carrying it out to the letter of the law! This is taken at the other end of Queen Street at the Drum Clock crossroads. On the right a sign, located high up on the wall, reveals that these are the premises of Timothy White Cash Chemists.

In the top right view, the corner properties, behind the fountain, are residential ones. They are still there but have been extended at ground level to make them into shops.

At the bottom right, the spire on, spire off, theme continues. Readers of the first Newton Abbot Album will recall that the spire was added in 1910, an 'inspirational' move to create a really noticeable landmark rising highly and heavenwards above the general level of town centre rooftops. This card was sent in 1921.

To continue our look at Queen Street we have two more views looking in opposite directions. The picture above is taken near the junction with King Street and the novelty of someone taking a photograph has brought out several children to see what is going on. On the right side of the photo to the left is a shop called Banbury's that is also shown, front on, on page 30. Beyond it, The Public Benefit Boot Company's shop is typical of the type that existed in those days displaying its items on the outside of the premises. Today it's doubtful that many shopkeepers would put their wares on such public show or even be allowed to do so.

27

Here we have two more Newton shops to show how times change. The one on the right is Coleman, the greengrocer and fruiterer, a shop that was in East Street opposite the Union Inn. Today Austin's occupy this site. Next door to it, on the left, was Lilly and Wills who were noted for their "Superfine Shag" or so it says in the photo. Above we have the Georgian-styled Newton Abbot Co-op that was established in 1880 but is represented, in this photo at least, by a very smart looking shop as it looked in 1948.
Opposite is a 1928 picture of a part of Queen Street complete with its earlier W. H. Smith & Son branch. On its right is Madge Mellor's cafe. The latter grew and expanded to establish itself as a well-known place to eat. Sadly it no longer exists and the shop is now an antique shop. W. H. Smith now trade at Courtenay Street and have one of the biggest shops in town.

These days, it's rare to find shops like this one of Banbury's anywhere other than in a museum of yesteryear. Each item was clearly priced to catch the eye of any passing, potential, customer. They were keen vendors of Kops' products, which included their Lemon Guenchlets and Kops' non-intoxicating ale and stout. J. Ford & Son, of 79 Queen Street, traded from these premises opposite the post office. The picture shows that they are butchers and various carcasses are shown here dangling. You probably had to 'duck' to enter the shop! Their advert stated that their specialities included Devon Ox Beef, Genuine Dairy-fed Pork and Wether Mutton – all at the best prices! The premises are still used for a butcher's shop, now that of Mr Saunders.

William Badcock & Sons' written advert in local guides and journals listed their activities as general drapers, tailors, outfitters and complete house furnishers. However above their wide premises they extended that range to include even more departments. Newton Abbot has many churches, some on high hills, closer to Heaven, others in the lower parts of the town. Opposite we have another three. Top left is St Paul's Church, which was built in 1863 in a cruciform shape, in a most pleasant setting at Devon Square. The money to finance this church came from the Earl of Devon.

St. Paul's Church, Newton Abbot

HIGHWEEK

Top right is the parish church of All Saints at Highweek. It was described by the late Professor Hoskins as "...heavily Victorianised and is of no great interest, but the views from the churchyard are worth seeing." However it has a long history that dates back to the thirteenth century when a Chapel-of-Ease, formerly by Kingsteignton, stood on the spot. This was because Highweek (Teignwick) was within the parish of Kingsteignton. The dead were carried along the Church Path for burial at the latter. The nature of the terrain, the likelihood of floods and the distance involved meant that funerals could well have been adventurous outings on occasions. In 1864 Highweek became a parish in its own right, and the church, despite the professor's comments, is beautiful inside and well looked after. To the left is the fifteenth century Wolborough Church dedicated to St Mary. The church is highly regarded for its great beauty within and the loveliness of its view without. Buried in the churchyard is John Lethbridge, the eighteenth century inventor of a diving machine. He was a remarkable man who made a fortune after salvaging precious items from sunken ships. With the vast sums of money that he made he purchased a large estate at Kingskerswell. Although he almost drowned on many occasions, he survived until he was 83, and was still diving almost up to the end!

Hospital, Newton Abbot

Decoy, Newton Abbot.

Newton Abbot, East Street

Here we have three cards of a similar type but showing three quite different views. The top left view is at Decoy, a part of Newton that has seen considerable change in recent years. Bottom left is a very quiet scene in East Street as it looked in 1908. Banberry's Dartmouth Inn is on the right side of the picture and the street has a far more relaxed about it than it does today.

Top right is a 1907 view of Newton Abbot Hospital. At that time it was set up by funds provided by generous benefactors and run by voluntary contributions. Once a year a carnival was staged with all the proceeds going to it. The carnival day was known as "Hospital Saturday" and many of the local hauliers would dress their horses in colourful plumes. They would polish the brasses 'til they gleamed. Even the chains, that these shire horses used to pull their loads, were given special treatment. Weeks before the big day they would be put into sacks. As the wheels turned the action would cause the chains to rub together polishing them up in the process. The end result were horses that caught the eye and stole the show. This picture shows off the architecture of the hospital and is not far from the sort of design that modern out-of-town hypermarkets seem to favour these days.

Here we have another hospital and the caption on the card states that it is "V A D Hospital". It was housed in Newton Hall, in Coach Road, and was used to help the injured and sick troops brought home from the First World War to convalesce. One of those injured young men is stood at the top of the flight of steps, his arm is in a sling. Many of the windows have been thrown open in order to air the rooms and a pair of onlookers are gazing out from a ground floor window. Following the Great War this large building was converted into flats. However it was later demolished to be replaced by a number of houses and maisonettes. A hark back to the past is evident in the fact that it's still known as Newton Hall.

In the first Newton Abbot Album there were several pictures of the swimming pool at Penn Inn and I'm glad to report that several swimmers of yesteryear came forward having recognised themselves or their friends and relations. This picture though predates those and shows work going on to get the swimming pool ready for its grand opening in 1934. The diving board, at the opposite deeper end, was presented by George Bidder, a local bookmaker, in memory of his daughter. The houses on the left are in Keyberry Road and the pool itself has been 'submerged' beneath a supermarket car park.

Although this picture is not pin sharp it's still worth including as it could never be taken again. Here we are looking, from the railway embankment, over the swimming pool at Penn Inn towards the point where the Penn Inn Roundabout is today. The nursery just beyond the pool was Tuplins which later became known as Milber Nursery. When the nursery was demolished The Church of Latter Day Saints was built on this site. The trees in the background formed an even more impressive backcloth than they do today.

Melba Village, Newton Abbot.

The postcard was incorrectly captioned by the postcard manufacturer concerned, a 'peach' of a mistake as it's Milber and not Melba! The bridge in the foreground is one that straddled Aller Brook and just beyond it would have the Penn Inn Roundabout. This card was posted from someone in Newton Abbot to a friend at Torquay in late August 1910 in an age when the journey between the two places would have seen little traffic. Another reminder, should we ever need one, how things have changed.

This is Penn Inn Park where the Plymco Supermarket is sited. At the thatched building, just right of centre, swimmers could purchase teas or ice creams. There was a lawn at the front with tables that saw plenty of use in fine summer weather. The houses on the right are part of the large residential area of Milber.

The picture above is a modern one but as change is almost inevitable in the years to come this view will alter just as the other older ones have done. This is taken from above Milber with the railway line giving the best indication on how to recognise the various places shown in the view. Decoy Lake just left above centre and Decoy's industrial estate is to the left of that whilst Milber's unusual church is in the lower centre. Many other landmarks can be seen and although there is a lot of built-up land there is still quite a bit of undeveloped countryside at the moment...

Some things change a lot and others ... well, they just remain in a timeless state. Courtenay Park's green and pleasant open spaces could, no doubt, tell many a story – those wonderful times as a child spent there years ago or that one last romantic kiss before a happy relationship was bridged by one of the duo leaving on the train to pastures new. Two of the views are similar but are separated by more than three score years and ten. The children by the fish pond are now pensioners! Much of the land between Newton's railway station and the town was owned by the Earl of Devon and the family name is, of course, Courtenay, a very commonly found one in Devon. Courtenay Park was laid out in 1854 at the same time the elegant houses and roads were developed in its vicinity and visitors arriving at Newton Abbot by train, for the first time would have been given an impression of a spacious, pleasant town.

Newton Abbot, Courtenay Park, the fish pond

This line up of the Auxiliary Fire service during the Second World War should revive a few memories for those who are still around. These men and women would have seen a lot of activity. The former Fire Station was based at the market and it's here that this picture was taken. If you look closely you will be able to spot a fire engine lurking behind the assembled group. The houses behind are in Halcyon Road.

Opposite are four pictures of Vicary's who operated in Bradley Lane. In the 1920s the firm were major employers with a workforce of about 700. Their activities included fellmongery, tanning and wool-combing. Three of the pictures depict a fire that raged through the factory in March 1920. The firm recovered from this disaster and continued in business until 1972.

41

Apart from sports teams, they don't take many pictures like this these days. Here we have an assembly of Newtonians captured for posterity, possibly in Courtenay Park, to celebrate a special occasion, perhaps a coronation. Newton Abbot's townspeople took advantage of rare public holidays to celebrate in style. A good example was the Coronation of Edward VII, in 1902. That was an event that saw two thousand people sitting down to eat in the park. On that occasion each child was, afterwards, presented with a box of chocolates and this in an age when this really was a treat. If you have any details about this particular event or the people involved I would like to know. The ladies in the assembled throng are in their summer best.

This photograph was taken by a Newton Abbot photographer called Brooks on the same occasion, and in the same location, as the one on the previous page, for the somewhat suave young gentleman with the boater, on the right of this picture, also appears in the one opposite and the one on the next page as well! He has contrived to maintain that slight tilt of his headwear. The lady sitting in the foreground is also in the last picture and wearing the same dress, although the lady beside her has cunningly disguised herself by removing her hat! There are more characters from the other view but we'll let you have the fun of working out which ones. This picture is a much more natural one and has a preponderance of young people, that is apart from the gent at the front who is looking away from the camera and who is sat on the all-important picnic hamper!

This is the last of the sequence of three that records a day out in the Newton area many years ago. Here we have an amalgamation of the characters involved on that day out when it appears to have been a fine day for them. If you look closely you will notice that the man in the middle, now also without his hat, has a football, of sorts, on his lap. The adage "Boys will be boys" is proven right here as three of them, in the back row, seem to be taking delight in thrusting sticks in front of their faces.

The last pages of this book are filled with pictures from a very special day for those old enough to recall it. V E Day (Victory in Europe) was celebrated on the 18 May 1945 not only in Newton Abbot but all across the realm. This picture of a street party was taken in Netley Road. Those on the next two pages were taken at Abbotsbury Road and Gladstone Place and feature a few familiar faces...

We end our second collection of nostalgic pictures with another photo from Gladstone Place. I hope that you have enjoyed this selection of pictures that feature people and places from a Newton Abbot of yesteryear. Just remember that if you are going to throw away any pictures like these, that you should really tell the 'bin man' first!